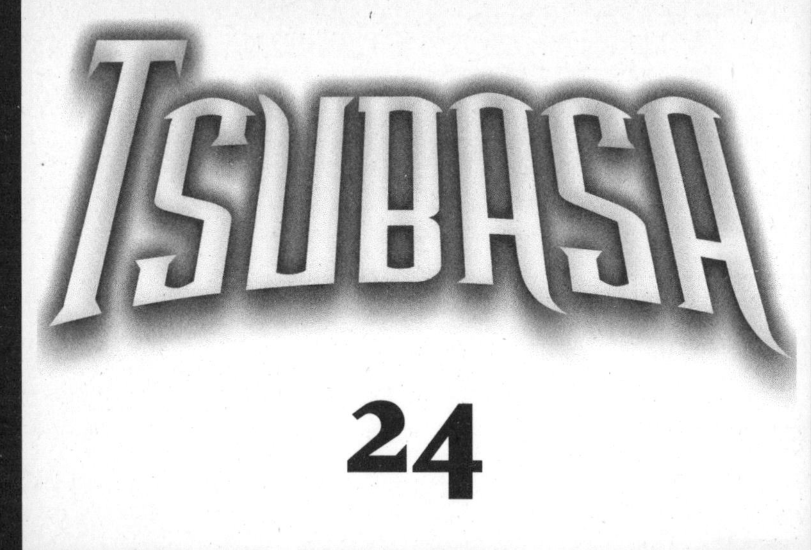

24

CLAMP

TRANSLATED AND ADAPTED BY
William Flanagan

LETTERED BY
Dana Hayward

BALLANTINE BOOKS • NEW YORK

Tsubasa, volume 24 is a work of fiction. Names, characters, places, and incidents are the products of the author's imagination or are used fictitiously. Any resemblance to actual events, locales, or persons, living or dead, is entirely coincidental.

A Del Rey Manga/Kodansha Trade Paperback Original

Published in the United States by Del Rey Books, an imprint of The Random House Publishing Group, a division of Random House, Inc., New York.

Publication rights arranged through Kodansha Ltd.

First published in Japan in 2008 by Kodansha Ltd., Tokyo

ISBN 978-0-345-51715-9

Printed in the United States of America

www.delreymanga.com

9 8 7 6 5 4 3 2 1

Translator/Adapter—William Flanagan
Lettering—Dana Hayward

Contents

Tsubasa crosses over with *xxxHOLiC*. Although it isn't necessary to read *xxxHOLiC* to understand the events in *Tsubasa*, you'll get to see the same events from different perspectives if you read both series!

Honorifics Explained

Throughout the Del Rey Manga books, you will find Japanese honorifics left intact in the translations. For those not familiar with how the Japanese use honorifics and, more important, how they differ from American honorifics, we present this brief overview.

Politeness has always been a critical facet of Japanese culture. Ever since the feudal era, when Japan was a highly stratified society, use of honorifics—which can be defined as polite speech that indicates relationship or status—has played an essential role in the Japanese language. When you address someone in Japanese, an honorific usually takes the form of a suffix attached to one's name (example: "Asuna-san"), is used as a title at the end of one's name, or appears in place of the name itself (example: "Negi-sensei," or simply "Sensei!").

Honorifics can be expressions of respect or endearment. In the context of manga and anime, honorifics give insight into the nature of the relationship between characters. Many English translations leave out these important honorifics and therefore distort the feel of the original Japanese. Because Japanese honorifics contain nuances that English honorifics lack, it is our policy at Del Rey not to translate them. Here, instead, is a guide to some of the honorifics you may encounter in Del Rey Manga.

-san: This is the most common honorific and is equivalent to Mr., Miss, Ms., or Mrs. It is the all-purpose honorific and can be used in any situation where politeness is required.

-sama: This is one level higher than "-san" and is used to confer great respect.

-dono: This comes from the word "tono," which means "lord." It is an even higher level than "-sama" and confers utmost respect.

-kun: This suffix is used at the end of boys' names to express familiarity or endearment. It is also sometimes used by men among friends, or when addressing someone younger or of a lower station.

-chan: This is used to express endearment, mostly toward girls. It is also used for little boys, pets, and even among lovers. It gives a sense of childish cuteness.

Bozu: This is an informal way to refer to a boy, similar to the English terms "kid" and "squirt."

Sempai/Senpai: This title suggests that the addressee is one's senior in a group or organization. It is most often used in a school setting, where underclassmen refer to their upperclassmen as "sempai." It can also be used in the workplace, such as when a newer employee addresses an employee who has seniority in the company.

Kohai: This is the opposite of "sempai" and is used toward underclassmen in school or newcomers in the workplace. It connotes that the addressee is of a lower station.

Sensei: Literally meaning "one who has come before," this title is used for teachers, doctors, or masters of any profession or art.

-[blank]: This is usually forgotten in these lists, but it is perhaps the most significant difference between Japanese and English. The lack of honorific means that the speaker has permission to address the person in a very intimate way. Usually, only family, spouses, or very close friends have this kind of permission. Known as *yobisute*, it can be gratifying when someone who has earned the intimacy starts to call one by one's name without an honorific. But when that intimacy hasn't been earned, it can be very insulting.

GO TO...
...THE KINGDOM OF CLOW!

Chapitre.183
The World of Sand

RESERVoir CHRoNiCLE

FWOOM
WHOOSH
AAAAAA

SHLUUM
VWAASAA

SHLUUM
POHH
SHLUUM
SHLUUM
GRMP

FASH
VZZT
VZZT

YÛKO!!
DOOM

NOW!
AAAAAAAA
PAAA

THANK YOU!
I PRAY THAT WHAT YOU CONSIDER MOST PRECIOUS IS RETURNED TO YOU.

SHLUUM

VWOOM

SSWOO
YÛKO!
WHOOSH
WAVER
YÛKO!

FROM HERE ON...
...THERE IS NOTHING MORE I CAN DO.
WHAT HAPPENS NOW...
...DEPENDS ENTIRELY ON WHAT THOSE CHILDREN... CHOOSE.

SO MY WORK GATHERING SOULS FROM THE DIMENSIONS HAS BETRAYED ME MORE THAN IT HAS HELPED.

BUT I HAVE MANAGED TO TAKE SOME SMALL REVENGE ON THE WITCH.
SHE WON'T BE ABLE TO TAKE PART IN THIS FOR QUITE A WHILE NOW.
ESPECIALLY WITHIN...

...THIS WORLD CUT OFF FROM TIME.
COME!
COME INTO MY WORLD!

FWMMP
MOKONA!
POFF
FINE...
MOKONA'S POWERS HAVE BEEN USED TO THE VERY LIMIT.
ARE YOU ALL RIGHT?
MOKONA JUST DID AS MUCH AS MOKONA COULD.

DID MOKONA GET US THERE...?
YES, YOU DID.

THIS IS THE KINGDOM OF CLOW!

RESERVoir CHRoNiCLE

Chapitre. 184
Cut Off From Time

The Kingdom of CLOW
BEYOND THAT GATE?
THERE'S A RESIDENTIAL DISTRICT, AND THE PALACE, BEYOND THAT.
BUT WHAT DOES IT MEAN TO BE CUT OFF FROM TIME?
I DON'T KNOW.
MAYBE IT MEANS THAT TIME'S STOPPED SOMEHOW.
EITHER THAT OR...

WHAT-
EVER IT
MEANS...
...THE THING
WE'RE LOOKING
FOR IS THAT WAY.
LET'S GO.
TAK
!!

CHATTER
ザワ
CHATTER
ザワ
CHATTER
ザワ
TMP
TMP
TMP
WHAT'S THIS...?
GRABB
AH!
GRICH

THANKS, MISTER!
SMILE
I REALLY MEAN IT! THANKS!
YOU'LL LIKE IT HERE! THE KINGDOM OF CLOW'S A GOOD PLACE!
ARE YOU A TRAVELER?
......
YES.

EVERYBODY LOOKS LIKE THEY'RE HAVING FUN.

CHATTER
ワイ
CHATTER
ワイ
......
SO WHAT IS THIS?
DO ANY OF YOU SENSE ANYTHING ODD ABOUT THE PEOPLE IN THIS CASTLE TOWN?

MOKONA WONDERS WHERE SAKURA IS.
ガヤ
MURMUR
ガヤ
MURMUR
HEY, MISTER!

THANKS FOR THE HELP BACK THERE!
I GOT ALL THE WAY HERE WITH-OUT SPILLING A SINGLE PIECE OF OUR STORE'S FRUIT THANKS TO YOU!
IT WAS NOTHING.

I WANT TO ADD MY THANKS AS WELL.
THERE'S NO CON-TROLLING MY BOY.

I DON'T SENSE ANY EVIL INTENT IN THEM...
...BUT IF THEY WANTED TO HIDE THEIR TRUE INTEN-TIONS, THEY PROBABLY COULD.
MUMBLE
WHISPER
.....
I IMAGINE YOU'RE RIGHT.
SST

SST
THOSE CLOTHES...
...ARE YOU FROM SOME OTHER COUNTRY?
YES.
WE ONLY ARRIVED JUST NOW...
...IN THE KINGDOM OF CLOW.

IT SEEMS LIKE THE THREE OF YOU ARE WEARING THREE VERY DIFFERENT OUTFITS.
DOES THAT MEAN YOU EACH COME FROM DIFFERENT COUNTRIES?

WE WERE BORN IN DIFFERENT COUNTRIES, BUT ...
...WE'VE BEEN TRAVELING TOGETHER FOR A LONG TIME.

THAT'S SO GREAT!
TRAVELING ALONE IS FUN, BUT I THINK IT'S BETTER GOING WITH OTHER PEOPLE.

.....
YES, I AGREE.

WELL, TAKE YOUR TIME WHILE YOU'RE HERE.
THE FESTIVAL IS COMING UP PRETTY SOON.
FESTIVAL?
YEAH!
OVER AT THE RUINS.

DO YOU HAVE A PLACE TO STAY ARRANGED?
NO, NOT YET...

THEN YOU SHOULD STAY WITH US!
YES, PLEASE! I INSIST.
WELL... I DON'T KNOW...

I THINK THAT'S A GOOD IDEA.
YOU'RE IN THE MIDDLE OF A JOURNEY, SO YOU SHOULD SAVE YOUR MONEY.
RIGHT?

BESIDES, THE NIGHTS IN THIS COUNTRY ARE REALLY COLD!
NOBODY COULD STAND SLEEPING OUTDOORS!

SST

IT'S TRUE. I THINK WE SHOULD SECURE A PLACE TO SLEEP FOR OURSELVES.

ALSO...
...SINCE WE STILL DON'T KNOW WHERE PRINCESS SAKURA IS...
...WE'LL NEED INFORMATION.
NOD
THE SUN'S ALREADY SETTING.

THANKS FOR DINNER!
IT WAS DELICIOUS!

YES, YOUR MOTHER IS AN EXCELLENT COOK.
YUP!
SHE ALSO MAKES THE BEST PAR-YU!

PAR-YU?
THESE HERE!
THEY'VE GOT THE APPLES WE SELL AT THE MARKET IN THEM!

HERE!

BE SURE TO TRY A PAR-YU TOMORROW MORNING.
SHFF

NOW, YOU MUST ALL BE VERY TIRED.
TAKE AS LONG A REST AS YOU NEED.
SKRRT
THANK YOU.

I TRIED TO ASK DURING DINNER, BUT...
...NOBODY SEEMS TO HAVE NOTICED ANYTHING ODD THAT HAPPENED RECENTLY.
IT PROBABLY MEANS THAT THE JERK HAS BEEN MOVING IN A WAY THE PEOPLE DON'T NOTICE, HUH?

GRIMP
......
I THINK WE SHOULD GO TO THE RUINS TO-MORROW.
THAT'S WHERE IT ALL STARTED.

CHEE
CHEE
CHEE
HUH?
SHFF
BOING
NOBODY'S HERE IN THE HOUSE.
PSSH
THEY WORK, SO THEY PROBABLY HAD TO LEAVE EARLY.

FSSH.
WHAT'S WRONG?
THE FOOD SHE MADE...

IT ISN'T HERE.
THE PAR-YU...
きょろ
GLANCE
DID KURO-GANE EAT IT ALL?
NO, I DIDN'T!
THINKING ABOUT THE WAY THE BOY AND HIS MOTHER ACTED LAST NIGHT...
...AS IF THE STUFF WAS PREPARED ESPECIALLY FOR OUR BREAKFAST. IT SEEMS A LITTLE STRANGE.
......
THAT'S TRUE.
MAYBE SOMETHING HAPPENED TO THEM.
TMP
WHOOSH

ぽす
GRIMP
きょろ
GLANCE

BOING
ぴょん

CHATTER
ザワ
CHATTER
ザワ
CHATTER
ザワ
TMP
TMP
TMP
AH!
GRICH
GRABB

THANKS, MISTER!
SMILE
I REALLY MEAN IT! THANKS!
YOU'LL LIKE IT HERE! THE KINGDOM OF CLOW'S A GOOD PLACE!
ARE YOU A TRAVELER?
...... YES.

EH?!

ツバサ
RESERVoir CHRoNiCLE

Chapitre. 185
Time in Repetition

.....
WHAT WAS THAT?

ガヤ
MURMUR
ガヤ
MURMUR

HEY, MISTER!

THANKS FOR THE HELP BACK THERE!
I GOT ALL THE WAY HERE WITHOUT SPILLING A SINGLE PIECE OF OUR STORE'S FRUIT THANKS TO YOU!
.....

I WANT TO ADD MY THANKS AS WELL.
THERE'S NO CONTROLLING MY BOY.

SST
......

SST
THOSE CLOTHES...
...ARE YOU FROM SOME OTHER COUNTRY?

IT SEEMS LIKE THE THREE OF YOU ARE WEARING THREE VERY DIFFERENT OUTFITS.
DOES THAT MEAN YOU EACH COME FROM DIFFERENT COUNTRIES?

THAT'S SO GREAT!

IT ISN'T JUST THE BOY!
EVERYONE IS SAYING THE VERY SAME THINGS THEY SAID YESTER-DAY!

WELL, TAKE YOUR TIME WHILE YOU'RE HERE.
THE FESTIVAL IS COMING UP PRETTY SOON.
FESTIVAL... YOU MEAN AT THE RUINS?

YEAH!
OVER AT THE RUINS.
......
DO YOU HAVE A PLACE TO STAY ARRANGED?
NO, NOT YET...

THEN YOU SHOULD STAY WITH US!
YES, PLEASE! I INSIST.

THE SUN'S ALREADY SETTING.

THIS IS WEIRD!
VERY LITTLE TIME HAS PASSED SINCE MOKONA AND EVERYBODY WOKE UP.

I THINK THAT'S A GOOD IDEA.
YOU'RE IN THE MIDDLE OF A JOUR-NEY, SO YOU SHOULD SAVE YOUR MONEY.
RIGHT?

DINNER WAS...
...DELICIOUS!

MOM ALSO MAKES THE BEST PAR-YU!

PAR-YU?
THESE HERE!
THEY'VE GOT THE APPLES WE SELL AT THE MARKET IN THEM!

MOKONA KNOWS...
MOKONA HEARD THAT LAST NIGHT...
ぽん
POFF

HERE!

SHFF
BE SURE TO TRY A PAR-YU TOMORROW MORNING.
NOW, YOU MUST ALL BE VERY TIRED.
TAKE AS LONG A REST AS YOU NEED.
SKRRT
THANK YOU.
FSSH
YES. IT'S ALL BEING REPEATED.

BUT IT ISN'T AN ENTIRE DAY.
IT'S ONLY A FEW HOURS FROM EARLY EVENING THROUGH THE NIGHT.
AND IT GETS REPEATED NO MATTER WHAT HAP-PENS.
POFF
ぽすっ
MOKONA WONDERS IF ANYTHING HAS CHANGED FROM BEFORE WE ALL GOT HERE?
MAYBE THE BOY WOULD HAVE FALLEN IF SYAORAN WASN'T THERE.

WHAT PURPOSE WOULD ANYBODY HAVE TO DO THIS?
WE DON'T KNOW...
...BUT...
...THE CHANCES ARE HIGH THAT THIS IS PART OF A PLOT BY FEI-WANG.

WHY DON'T WE...
...TEST THIS FOR ONE MORE DAY?
AND FIND OUT IF TOMORROW IS JUST AS LONG AS TODAY WAS.
......YES.
SHFF
YOU DIDN'T SLEEP IN A DIFFERENT ROOM FROM THE KID YESTERDAY. WHAT'S YOUR REASON FOR DOING IT TONIGHT?

I'M CERTAIN YOU NOTICED ALSO.

......

WHOOSH
OR, TO BE MORE PRECISE, I SHOULD SAY THAT I FIGURE THAT YOU HAD REALIZED...

...THAT I HAD NOTICED.

LLPP
EVER SINCE MY BODY CHANGED INTO THIS ONE, MY SENSE OF SMELL FOR BLOOD HAS BECOME PRETTY SHARP.

ALSO...
...EVEN THOUGH YOU'RE INSIDE A WARM ROOM, THE FACT THAT YOU DON'T REMOVE YOUR CLOAK OR HEADPIECE...
...IS SOMEWHAT UNNATURAL.

I ASSUME IT'S TO HIDE YOUR EXPRESSION.
THAT YOU'RE BEARING A LOT OF PAIN.
.....
DOES YOUR PROSTHETIC ARM...NOT QUITE FIT?
I CAN MOVE IT. SO THERE'S NO PROBLEM.
DOES IT HURT MORE THAN YESTERDAY?
.....

ANSWER ME!
THIS MAY BE A WAY OF BEING SURE THAT WHILE TIME IN THE KINGDOM OF CLOW IS REPEATING, OUR TIME IS MOVING FORWARD.

TSK!
.....
YEAH.
AS WE TRAVEL TOGETHER, THERE ARE MORE AND MORE THINGS WE CAN'T HIDE.
AND IT WILL BE WORSE FOR SYAORAN-KUN AND MOKONA WHEN THEY FIND OUT LATER.
SLAMM
IF IT HURTS, THEN SAY IT HURTS FROM THE START!
IDIOT!
YOU JERK!

TSK!
ちっ
......
YOU'RE ONE TO TALK!
IT'S BE-CAUSE IT'S ME THAT I CAN TALK!
GRIMP
CAN'T SYAORAN SLEEP?
I'M WONDER-ING AT WHAT MOMENT TIME STARTS OVER.
I WAS HOPING TO FIND THE EXACT TIME...

SLUMP
. . . . .
WHAT WAS THAT?
MOKONA'S EYES CAN'T STAY OPEN...
PLIP
ROLLLLL

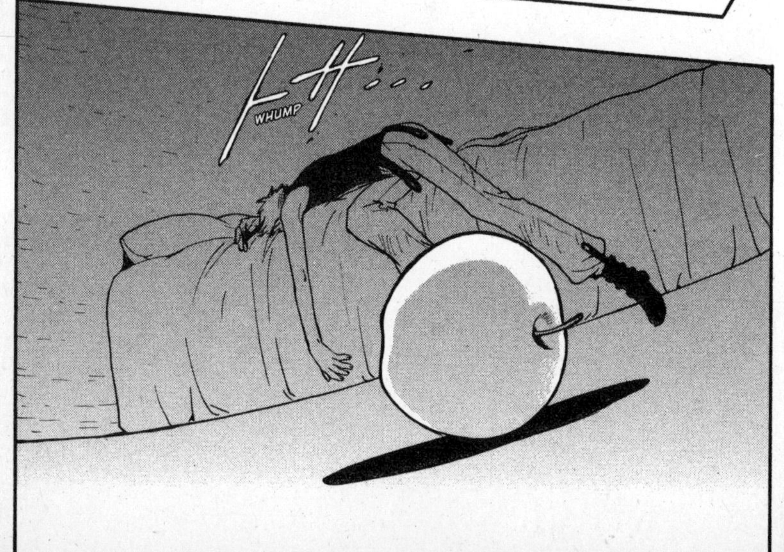
WHUMP

CHEE
CHEE
CHEE
FAI? KURO-GANE?
DID FAI AND KUROGANE SUDDENLY GET SLEEPY LAST NIGHT?
THE SAME HAPPENED TO YOU TWO AS WELL?
KREEE

CHATTER
ザワ
CHATTER
ザワ
CHATTER
ザワ

IT'S ONLY REPLAYING A FIXED AMOUNT OF TIME FROM THE EARLY EVENING TO SOME POINT AT NIGHT.
TMP
TMP
TMP

AH!
GRICH
GRABB

THANKS, MISTER!
SMILE
ARE YOU A TRAVELER?
.....
I REALLY MEAN IT! THANKS!
YOU'LL LIKE IT HERE! THE KINGDOM OF CLOW'S A GOOD PLACE!
IT'S AS IF SOME PLAN OF FEI-WANG'S...
...IS FORCING THESE PEOPLE TO REPLAY THE SAME EVENTS OVER AND OVER...!!

Chapitre. 186
Time That Does Not Advance

THESE PEOPLE'S LIVES AREN'T ADVANCING AT ALL...
...THAT'S WHAT THIS MEANS, HUH?

NO MATTER HOW LONG THEY WAIT, TOMORROW WILL NEVER COME.
THERE'S SOMETHING ABOUT IT THAT MAKES MOKONA VERY SAD.

HEY, MISTER!

THANKS FOR THE HELP BACK THERE!
I GOT ALL THE WAY HERE WITHOUT SPILLING A SINGLE PIECE OF OUR STORE'S FRUIT THANKS TO YOU!

......

I WANT TO ADD MY THANKS AS WELL.
THERE'S NO CONTROLLING MY BOY.

BUT THERE ARE PEOPLE...
...FOR WHOM THE ADVANCEMENT OF TIME MAY BE SADDER THAN IF TIME HAD STOPPED.
WHAT'S THAT MEAN?
FOR EXAMPLE...

...IF A LITTLE AFTER THESE HOURS... SOMETHING WERE TO HAPPEN.

THOSE CLOTHES...
...ARE YOU FROM SOME OTHER COUNTRY?
THEY'RE SAYING THE SAME THINGS...
...BUT THERE ARE CHANGES.
LIKE WHAT?
THERE ARE FEWER PEOPLE.

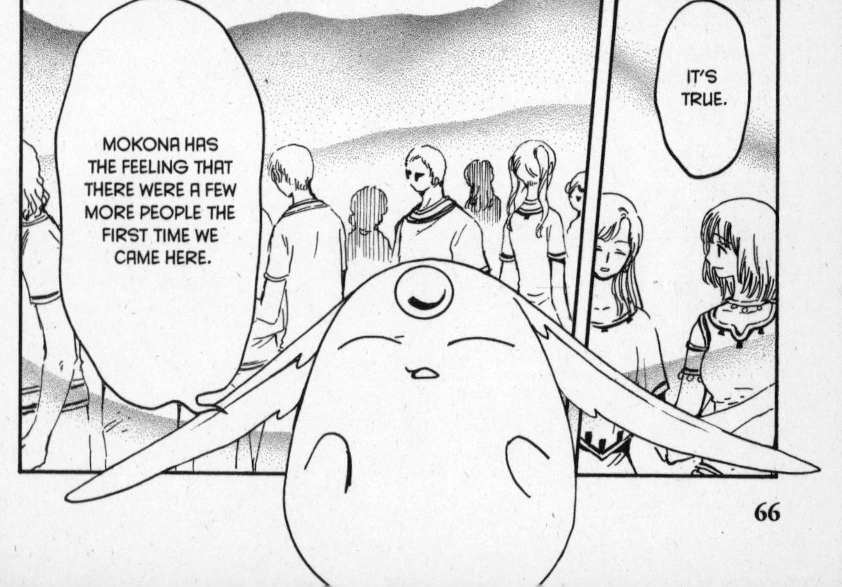

IT'S TRUE.
MOKONA HAS THE FEELING THAT THERE WERE A FEW MORE PEOPLE THE FIRST TIME WE CAME HERE.

IT SEEMS LIKE THE THREE OF YOU ARE WEARING THREE VERY DIFFERENT OUTFITS.
DOES THAT MEAN YOU EACH COME FROM DIFFERENT COUNTRIES?

THAT'S SO GREAT!

I SEE IT TOO.

RIGHT NOW, SOMEBODY SAID, "TRAVELING ALONE IS FUN, BUT I THINK IT'S BETTER GOING WITH OTHER PEOPLE."
THAT PERSON ISN'T HERE.

......

WELL, TAKE YOUR TIME WHILE YOU'RE HERE.
THE FESTIVAL IS COMING UP PRETTY SOON.

......
WHAT IS THE FESTIVAL FOR?

IT'S A FESTIVAL TO CELEBRATE THE BIRTHDAY OF THE KING'S DAUGHTER, PRINCESS SAKURA!

PRINCESS SAKURA? DOES THAT MEAN SAKURA?!
THE PRINCESS MEANS THE PRINCESS!
SHE'S SO CUTE!
SHE TRULY IS A CHARMING YOUNG PRINCESS.
JUST WHEN...
...IN CLOW'S HISTORY IS THIS?
SAKURA...
THE PRINCESS... HOW OLD WILL SHE BE ON THIS BIRTHDAY?

NOW LET ME SEE...
THE BIRTHDAY COMING UP MAKES HER...
...SEVEN YEARS OLD!
AH!
THAT MEANS THAT THIS IS IN CLOW'S PAST, HUH?
EVEN IF WE WANTED TO CONFIRM IT, WE'LL NEVER FIND OUT THE TRUTH HERE.

WE'LL HAVE TO GO TO THE CASTLE TO SEE SAKURA, WON'T WE?
THE PRINCESS ISN'T IN THE CASTLE RIGHT NOW.

BEFORE HER BIRTH-DAY, SHE HAS TO...
WHAT'S IT CALLED?
PURIFICA-TION.
THAT'S IT! SHE HAS TO DO THAT THING AT THE RUINS!
......
SAKU-RA...
THIS IS WHEN...
I SHOULD HAVE KNOWN.
"SHOULD HAVE KNOWN"...?

DO YOU HAVE A PLACE TO STAY AR-RANGED?
THEN YOU SHOULD STAY WITH US!
YES, PLEASE!
......
DLUUP

SHLUU
UUUUUUUU

KACHIK

I THINK THAT'S A GOOD IDEA.
YOU'RE IN THE MIDDLE OF A JOURNEY...
DUUUP

BLISH
?!
WHOOSH
BESIDES, THE NIGHTS IN THIS COUNTRY ARE REALLY COLD!
NOBODY COULD STAND SLEEPING OUTDOORS!
......

WHAT?!
WHAT'S GOING ON?!
SHAKK
WHY ARE THE PEOPLE SUD-DENLY...?!
MOKONA DIDN'T... NONE OF US DID ANY-THING!!

NO, WE DID DO SOME-THING.
WE CHANGED THINGS.
THE PEOPLE INSIDE THIS WORLD LIVED THE DAY OVER AND OVER WITHOUT A CHANGE. BUT WE APPEARED AND CHANGED IT.
AH!
MOKONA WONDERS IF ANYTHING HAS CHANGED FROM BEFORE WE ALL GOT HERE?
MAYBE THE BOY WOULD HAVE FALLEN IF SYAORAN WASN'T THERE.
B-BUT...
DLUUP
WHY WOULD THEY MELT?!
SHH
SHH
......
SO THIS IS WHY THERE WERE FEWER PEOPLE!

THESE PEOPLE... ARE ALIVE, AREN'T THEY?
AT THE VERY LEAST, THEY WEREN'T A FORM OF ILLUSION.
BUT DOES THAT MEAN...
...THAT MOKONA AND THE REST OF US DID SOMETHING TO MAKE THIS HAPPEN TO THESE PEOPLE?!
GRNND

ツバサ
RESERVoir CHRoNiCLE

Chapitre. 187
The Punishment for a Wish

THE PEOPLE WITHIN THIS DIMENSION CUT OFF FROM TIME...
...HAVE REPEATED THE ACTIONS IN THOSE SAME HOURS OVER AND OVER...
...AND AS SUCH, WERE ALIVE.
THIS REPETITION OF THE SAME EVENTS...
...THIS LACK OF FORWARD MOVEMENT ENSURED THEIR EXISTENCE.

AND SO...
...WHEN THEY CON-FRONT AN EXISTENCE THAT DOES NOT REPEAT...
...THEIR EQUILIB-RIUM IS DESTROYED.
THE MORE THE NEW EXIS-TENCE AP-PROACHES...
...IN ITS EFFORT TO SEEK NEW INFOR-MATION.
...THE MORE LIVES WITHIN THE CUT-OFF SPACE-TIME ARE LOST.

SHHAA
SHHSH

LET'S GET TO THE RUINS!
SHHH
THAT'S WHERE SAKURA IS!
MAYBE, BUT...
...WHICH SAKURA-CHAN?

THE SAKURA THAT I MET!
YOU MEAN...
...THROUGH THE EYES OF THE OTHER...
NO! I DON'T MEAN THAT!

THE SAKURA I WAS WITH...
...UNTIL THE DAY I WAS TAKEN.

DMP

HEY, MISTER! WHERE ARE YOU AND YOUR FRIENDS GOING?

IT ISN'T SAFE OUTSIDE OF TOWN!

COME STAY WITH US!

COME STAY WITH US!

DLUUUP
COME STAY WITH US!

COME STAY WITH US!
COME STAY WITH US!
COME STAY WITH US!
SHHAA
AAAA
DLUUP
DLUUP
CAN THESE PEOPLE EVER GO BACK TO THE WAY THEY WERE?!
ARE THEY GOING TO DIE LIKE THIS?!
SHHAA

MISTER! AND ALL OF YOU!
COME STAY WITH US!
MOM'S COOKING IS REALLY GREAT!
DWUP

IF YOU DON'T MOVE FORWARD, IT'S THE SAME AS BEING DEAD.
I'M GOING...
I'M GOING TO TRY TO FULFILL A WISH!
BUT THE ACTIONS I TAKE FROM NOW ON...
...ARE NO JUSTIFICATION FOR WHAT I'VE JUST DONE TO YOU!
BUT I'LL TAKE THE PUNISHMENT... ALL OF IT UPON MYSELF!

SST

PLIP
PLIP
SHK

SHE TAKES APPLES...
...AND MAKES PAR-YU OUT OF THEM!
I JUST KNOW YOU'RE GOING TO LOVE IT!

COME STAY WITH US!
SHK
COME STAY WITH... US...!
SHK

...
YOU'LL INJURE YOURSELF.
SST
KLNCH

YOU'RE RIGHT. IF A PERSON LIVES INSIDE TIME THAT DOESN'T MOVE FORWARD, IT'S JUST LIKE A LIVING DEATH.
ZHHHH-HHH
BE-SIDES...
SHK
SHK
...IF YOU'RE GUILTY OF SOMETHING, THEN I'M JUST AS GUILTY.
ZHHHHHHHH
AS AM I.
MOKONA IS TOO!
SHK
SHK

......
THANK YOU.
ALL WHO MAKE WISHES ARE THE SAME.
WHEN ONE'S WISH COMES INTO CONFLICT WITH SOMEONE ELSE'S WISH...
...THEN ONE MUST MAKE A CHOICE
EITHER ABANDON ONE'S OWN WISH...
...OR CRUSH THE OTHER'S WISH FOR THE SAKE OF YOUR OWN.
AT THIS MOMENT, I SAW YOU...
...TURN YOUR BACK ON THE PEOPLE OF THE TOWN FOR THE SAKE OF YOUR OWN WISH.

WE ARE THE SAME...
...AS LONG AS WE WISH.

ツバサ
RESERVoir CHRoNiCLE

Chapitre. 188

The Ruins on That Day

SHK
SHK
ぷるぷる
TRMBL
TRMBL
FSH
THANKS.
LET'S GO QUICKLY.
SHK
SHK
IN ONLY A LITTLE MORE TIME, WE'LL SUDDENLY GET SLEEPY.
AND TIME WILL TURN BACK AGAIN.

......
NO.
ONCE WE'RE IN THE RUINS...
...I DOUBT THAT WILL HAPPEN AGAIN.

HOW DO YOU KNOW?
SHK
IF MY REASONING IS CORRECT...
TIME IN THE RUINS...

...WILL PROBABLY BE STOPPED...
...ON THAT DAY.
KREEE

KREEEEE
EEEE
IT OPENED ON ITS OWN...!
AS IF IT'S WEL-COMING US.
JUST HOW I LIKE IT!

TAK

ISN'T...
...ANY-BODY HERE?

THE ONLY PEOPLE ALLOWED IN THE RUINS DURING THE PURIFICATION RITES ARE THE HIGH PRIEST...
...AND THE MEMBER OF THE ROYAL FAMILY TAKING PART IN THE CEREMONY.

BY "MEMBER OF THE ROYAL FAMILY," YOU MEAN THE SAKURA-CHAN...
...THAT YOU KNEW?

......
YEAH.

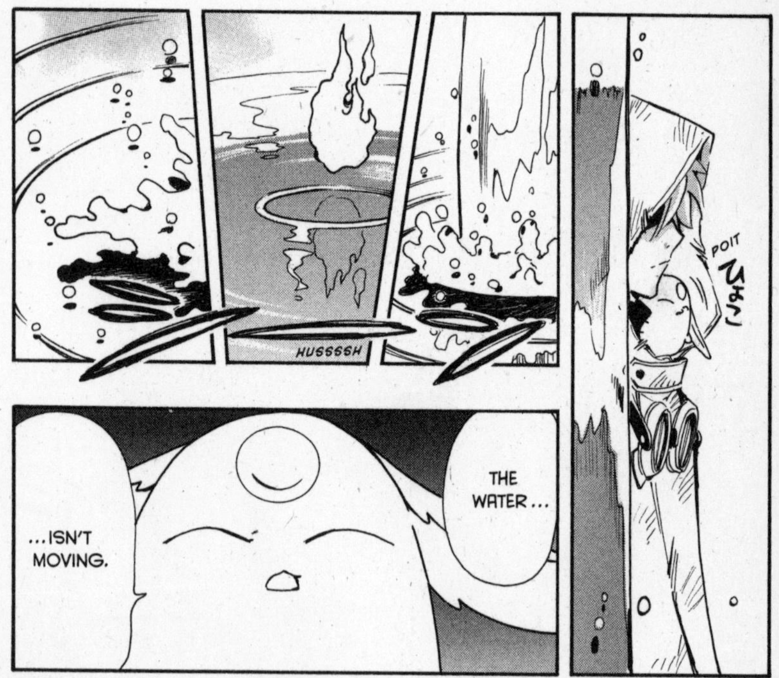
POIT
HUSSSSH
THE WATER...
...ISN'T MOVING.

IN THE MIDDLE OF A DESERT, ALL THIS WATER...
IT SPEAKS, OF COURSE, OF GREAT CON-STRUCTION SKILLS...
...BUT ALSO A GOOD DEAL OF MAGICAL POWER IS BEING USED TO SUPPORT THIS PLACE.
SHH
TIME REALLY IS STOPPED, ISN'T IT?
NOT TO MENTION ITS MAINTENANCE AND THAT OF THE BUILDING AROUND IT.
YES.
THAT IS ONE OF THE VITAL DUTIES PERFORMED BY THIS COUNTRY'S HIGH PRIEST.
ALSO, SINCE SAKURA...
...HAD THE GREATEST MAGICAL POWER OF ANYONE IN THE ROYAL FAMILY AT THE TIME...
...SHE WAS SET TO BECOME THE NEXT HIGH PRIEST...

HOW LONG WAS SYAORAN WITH SAKURA?
......
ALWAYS.
EH?
WE WERE ALWAYS TOGETHER.
FROM THE TIME WE MET...
...SEVEN DAYS BEFORE OUR SEVENTH BIRTHDAYS...

...UNTIL MY BODY REACHED THIS AGE AND FORM.
ALWAYS.
B- BUT...
...SYAORAN WAS TAKEN...
...WHEN SYAORAN WAS LITTLE!

I TURNED BACK TIME...
...BY PAYING A PRICE.
......
YOU MEAN TO THE WITCH?
YES.
TO YÛKO?
WOULD YOU MIND TELLING US WHY?

I WANTED TO RETURN SAKURA...
...TO THAT DAY.

RESERVoir CHRoNiCLE

Chapitre. 189
An Inherited Mental Preparation

.....
SO THIS IS THE PLACE?
TMP

WELCOME TO THE SHOP!
IS THIS...
...WHERE THE ONE CALLED THE TIME-SPACE WITCH IS?
MISTRESS, A CUSTOMER!
MISTRESS, A CUSTOMER!
JUST A MINUTE!
I WAS JUST TOLD TO COME HERE, BUT...
I DON'T KNOW...
YANK
YANK
YOU DO NOT NEED TO KNOW.

YOUR VISITING THIS SHOP...
...IS HITSUZEN.

......
HITSUZEN.
WHAT IS YOUR NAME?
......
LI SYAO-RAN.
YOU HAVE THE SAME NAME AS YOUR FATHER, HM?
AND YOU DO NOT REVEAL YOUR TRUE NAME ... YES?

IT SEEMS THAT SYAORAN TAUGHT YOU WELL.
QUITE A FEW THINGS.
YOU KNOW MY FATHER?
AND YOUR MOTHER.
SAKURA-CHAN.
HOW-EVER...
...I HAVE NEVER MET THEM.
NOW...
THIS IS A STORE THAT GRANTS WISHES.
THE VERY FACT THAT YOU HAVE ENTERED THE STORE...
...MEANS THAT YOU HAVE A WISH.

SO, WHAT IS...
...YOUR WISH?
I DON'T HAVE ONE!
NONE?
IF I HAVE ANY WISHES, I'LL FULFILL THEM MYSELF!
BUT...
...YOU'VE COME IN HERE.
MY FATHER...

...TOLD YOU TO COME TO MY SHOP.
DID HE TELL YOU WHY?
コク
NOD
MY MOTHER HAD A DREAM.
SHE SAID THAT THERE WAS SOMEBODY WAITING FOR ME.
SAKURA-CHAN HAS HAD THE ABILITY TO SEE THE FUTURE IN DREAMS FOR A LONG TIME.
......

. . . . . VERY WELL.
SO WHAT WILL YOU DO?
I'M GOING!
HAVE YOU LEARNED . . .
. . . WHERE THIS PERSON IS?
IN SOME WORLD DIFFERENT FROM HERE IN JAPAN.
THAT'S WHAT MY FATHER SAID.
YES.
A COUNTRY IN A VERY DIFFERENT WORLD.
AND WHAT IS YOUR METHOD TO CROSS DIMENSIONS?
I DON'T HAVE ONE.
AND EVEN SO . . . ?
I'M GOING!

IF THERE'S ANYTHING THAT I CAN DO...
...I'M GOING TO DO IT!
YOU ARE EXACTLY LIKE YOUR FATHER.
YOUR WISH SHALL BE GRANTED.

I HEARD THAT A PRICE HAS TO BE PAID TO HAVE A WISH GRANTED.
SST
AS TO THE PRICE, I HAVE ALREADY RECEIVED IT...
...FROM YOUR MOTHER.

ARE YOU READY?
BOTH YOUR MIND AND WILL PREPARED?
FWOONN
NOD
コク
VERY WELL...
...THEN GO!

MAKE CHOICES...
...AS YOUR BELIEFS DICTATE.
?!
SHLOOM

KEEEEE
TMP
WHERE AM I?
AM I IN THE KINGDOM OF CLOW THAT MOTHER DREAMED ABOUT?

.....
WHO...
...ARE YOU?

ツバサ
RESERVoir CHRoNiCLE

Chapitre.190
Those Who Know the World

WHO ARE YOU?
AH!
TAK
MY NAME IS...
...SYA—
WHOOSH
WAIT...!
ZUBLASSH

SPUSH
SPUSH
SPUSH
TWITCH
NO!
SST
...BUT...
...IT'S FORBIDDEN TO TOUCH ME.
I'M SORRY...

SPISH
I'M SORRY.
I'M RIGHT IN THE MIDDLE OF A PURIFICATION RITE IN THIS POOL.
NOBODY'S ALLOWED TO TOUCH ME.
PLASH
PLASH
PURIFI-CATION...
SO YOU HAVE SOME IMPORTANT CEREMONY TO CON-DUCT?
AH!
...... WHAT?
I JUST NEVER EXPECTED ANYBODY ELSE TO KNOW THAT PURIFICA-TION IS DONE...
...BEFORE IMPORTANT CEREMONIES.
I'VE DONE IT MYSELF A NUMBER OF TIMES.
REALLY? YOU HAVE?

YOUR CLOTHES... YOU'RE NOT FROM CLOW, ARE YOU?
SO YOU CAME FROM SOME OTHER COUNTRY?
......
SOME OTHER WORLD.
OTHER...
...WORLD...?
YEAH.
I CAME HERE FROM A COUNTRY NAMED JAPAN IN A DIFFERENT DIMENSION.

JAPAN...
IT DOESN'T SHOCK YOU?
I'VE HEARD OF IT BEFORE.
FROM MOTHER-SAMA...
...WHO IS ALSO THE HIGH PRIESTESS.

I WAS TOLD...
...IF A PERSON KNOWS THE NATURE OF THE WORLD...
...THEN THAT PER-SON KNOWS THERE ISN'T ONLY ONE WORLD.
I WAS TOLD THE SAME THING...
...BY MY MOTHER.

BUT IT'S AN ODD THING.
JAPAN AND THE KING-DOM OF CLOW ARE TWO COMPLETELY DIFFERENT WORLDS, BUT WE CAN STILL TALK TO EACH OTHER.
THAT'S A BIG COINCI-DENCE...
NO.
THERE IS NO CO-INCIDENCE IN THIS WORLD.
THE ONLY THING IS HITSUZEN.
DID YOUR MOTHER-SAMA SAY THAT TOO?

NO.
MY FATHER.
HITSU-ZEN...
MAYBE MY MEETING YOU IS HITSUZEN TOO!

TELL ME YOUR NAME.
......
...... LI SYAORAN.
I'M SAKURA OF THE KINGDOM OF CLOW.
THE SAME NAME AS MY MOTHER...
EH?
STARE

THEY LOOK ALIKE!
JUST LIKE MY MOTHER WHEN SHE WAS YOUNG.
?
SST
WEREN'T YOU IN THE MIDDLE OF A PURIFICA-TION RITE?

MOTHER-SAMA!
SHE DOES TOO...
SHE LOOKS JUST LIKE MY MOTHER'S MOTHER WHO I SAW IN THE PHOTO-GRAPHS...

YOU SEEM TO BE HAV-ING FUN, PRINCESS SAKURA.
I-I'M SORRY!
BUT... BUT I'M STILL UNTOUCHED LIKE I VOWED TO BE!
REALLY I AM!
ALL I DID WAS FALL OVER IN THE POOL!
BUT... BUT!!
WA WA WA
はわわ
I KNOW. DON'T WORRY.
WELCOME TO THE KINGDOM OF CLOW.
TRAVELER FROM ANOTHER WORLD.
HOW DID YOU KNOW...
FROM A DREAM.

YOU'RE A DREAM SEER TOO?
にこ
SMILE
GRRL
GRRRRL
じた
PANIC
じた
PANIC
THAT WAS JUST…
UM… UM…

WELL, OF COURSE IT'S EVEN-ING TIME.
AND THE PURIFICATION DUTIES ARE FINISHED FOR THE DAY, SO LET'S RETIRE TO THE CASTLE.
ALSO, WE HAVE A FAVORITE OF PRINCESS SAKURA, APPLES, AT THE READY.
HOO
はうー
LET US ALL GO.
BUT...
OF COURSE WE HAVE YOUR PLACE AT THE TABLE PREPARED AS WELL.
YOU ARE FOND OF FRUITS, YES?

SO IT'S TRUE! THIS PERSON ALSO...
...CAN SEE THE FUTURE IN DREAMS!

TMP
TMP
LET'S GO EAT TO-GETHER!
OKAY?
O-OKAY...
YAAY!
AH...
GLOOB
KER-WHUMP
AHH!

IT'S OVER HERE!
IS THIS REALLY A CASTLE?
ARE CASTLES SO DIFFERENT IN JAPAN?

WE HAVE DESERTS IN JAPAN, BUT...
...THIS IS A LOT DIFFERENT FROM ANY PLACE I'VE BEEN TO.
PRINCESS SAKURA!

FATHER-
SAMA!

とTMP
とTMP
とTMP
YOU'RE GOING TO HAVE TO RESTRAIN YOURSELF, AT LEAST FOR SIX MORE DAYS UNTIL THE PURIFICATION RITE IS OVER.
YES...
...FATHER-SAMA.
ぴた
STP
CAN I BEG YOU FOR AN INTRODUCTION?
WE MET AT THE PURIFICATION POOL AT THE RUINS!
SST
I AM LI SYAORAN.

I'M FUJITAKA, KING OF CLOW.

I IMAGINE YOU BOTH ARE HUNGRY.

WE'LL SAVE THE TALK FOR AFTER.

へこ NOD

LET'S GO!

......

SO HE'S THE ONE, HM?

YES.
HE IS PRINCESS SAKURA'S DESTINY.

Chapitre. 191
The Seven-Day Promise

HE IS THE ONE AROUND WHOM PRINCESS SAKURA'S DESTINY REVOLVES.
AND...
...THE FUTURE CHANGES...
THE PRINCESS'S AND THAT BOY'S FATE WILL BE CHANGED.
LET'S PLACE OUR TRUST...
...IN THOSE CHILDREN.
......
YES, YOU'RE RIGHT.

H-HAVE A SEAT.
I KNEW IT!
WHAT DID YOU KNOW?

I'M STILL IN THE MIDDLE OF PURIFICATION, SO I'M ONLY ALLOWED TO EAT THINGS LIKE FRUITS AND HERBS...
...BUT LOOK!
THERE'S MEAT AND PURIA...
...AND THEY HAVE COCOTTO THERE TOO!
MOTHER-SAMA SAW YOUR COM-ING IN A DREAM AND MADE SURE YOUR MEAL WAS PREPARED!
AMAZING...

MY MOTHER HAS THE ABILITY TO SEE THE FUTURE IN DREAMS TOO.
BUT SHE SAID SHE HARDLY HAD ANY FUTURE DREAMS EVER SINCE A LITTLE BEFORE I WAS BORN.
IS THAT SO?
?
MY MOTHER'S NAME IS ALSO...
...SAKURA.
EH...?

AND... YOU LOOK LIKE HER.
YOU LOOK JUST LIKE MY MOTHER WHEN SHE WAS YOUNG.
I DO?
YES.
IT'S JUST A COINCI-DENCE.
OR MAYBE IT ISN'T, HUH?
MAYBE THAT WAS HITSUZEN TOO.
.....

BUT...
...MY NAME IS...
EH?
ふる
SHAKE
CAN I CALL YOU SYAORAN?
.....

......YES.
......SYAORAN!

BA-BAMM
SOMEBODY WAS IN THE PURIFICATION ROOM?!
BIG BROTHER TÔYA-SAMA! YUKITO-SAN!

STOMP
STOMP
......
SO IT WAS THIS BRAT?
BZZT
BZZT
TÔYA-SAMA!
HUMPH
TÔYA...
AWW...

GOOD EVENING.
GOOD EVENING.
BOW
I HAVE THE FEELING THIS ISN'T THE FIRST TIME WE'VE MET.
YOU ARE EXACTLY LIKE THE ONE I DREAMED OF.
YOU'RE A DREAM SEER TOO?
YES, BUT I ONLY SAW THE SLIGHTEST BIT.
JUST THE EXCHANGE WE'RE HAVING NOW.
YUKITO-SAN IS SECOND ONLY TO MOTHER-SAMA . . .
. . . IN MAGICAL POWER IN THE KING-DOM.
EVERYBODY IN THE CLERGY ALL SAY SO, DON'T THEY?
THAT ISN'T TRUE.
IF WE INCLUDE DORMANT POWER, THEN PRINCESS SAKURA'S POWERS FAR OUTSTRIP MINE.

BUT I'VE NEVER SEEN THE FUTURE IN A DREAM.
I CAN'T DO ANY-THING!
THE LITTLE POWER I HAVE IS A FEELING FOR LIVING THINGS.
A FEELING FOR LIVING THINGS?
YOU KNOW, LIKE TREES AND FLOWERS...
...AND BIRDS AND STUFF.
BUT...
...THE THING I UNDER-STAND THE MOST IS THE FEELING OF WATER!
......
THAT ISN'T "A LITTLE"!

EH?
TO BE ABLE TO UNDER-STAND THE FEELINGS OF THINGS THAT CAN'T SPEAK FOR THEMSELVES...
THAT ISN'T "A LITTLE" POWER!
I THINK IT'S AMAZING!!

THANK... YOU!
BLUSH
START EATING!
BRAT!
KEEEEN
BZZT
BZZT
......
I'M SORRY...
...ABOUT BROTHER-SAMA.
IT'S OKAY.
HE'S ALWAYS TEASING...
...BUT TODAY WAS A LOT WORSE THAN NORMAL.

むすっ
MLOOB
SAY...
...SYAO-RAN...
ぽぽ
POP
POP
ぱっ
POP
WHAT?
CAN YOU STAY IN MY COUNTRY ALWAYS?
FOR THIS FIRST TRANSFER, YOU WILL ONLY BE ALLOWED TO STAY IN THE KINGDOM OF CLOW...
...FOR SEVEN DAYS.
ONCE THAT PERIOD IS OVER, YOU MUST RETURN TO YOUR ORIGINAL WORLD BEFORE BEING ABLE TO GO AGAIN.

WHAT YOU DO AFTER-WARD...
...IS A CHOICE YOU MUST MAKE.
SEVEN DAYS.
AND WHEN THAT'S OVER...
...WILL YOU COME BACK?
I...
...DON'T KNOW YET.

I SUPPOSE YOUR MOTHER-SAMA AND FATHER-SAMA ARE WAITING FOR YOU, HUH?
OH, YEAH!
DO YOU ALREADY HAVE A PLACE TO STAY FOR YOUR SEVEN DAYS?
THEN HOW ABOUT STAYING HERE?!
BUT...
HUH?
NO...
I'M SURE FATHER-SAMA AND MOTHER-SAMA WILL GIVE THEIR APPROVAL!
AND IF TÔYA-SAMA TRIES TO BULLY YOU, HE'LL HAVE ME TO DEAL WITH!
BIG BROTHER-SAMA CAN'T DEFEAT ME!

YOU'RE VERY BRAVE, HUH?
SO...
...YOU'LL STAY IN THE CASTLE?

THANK YOU!

I'M NOT ALLOWED TO TOUCH YOU...

...BUT THIS ISN'T AGAINST THE RULES!

PAFF
THAT SOUNDS GOOD.
FWAAA

......
YEAH.
THANK YOU!
I'M SUP-POSED TO BE THE ONE THANKING YOU.
ぽっ
POP
BUT I'M SO HAPPY!
I'LL BE IN THE CASTLE EVERY MINUTE THAT I'M NOT AT THE PURIFICATION RITES!
I CAN'T SHOW YOU THROUGH THE TOWN, BUT I CAN BE WITH YOU ALL THE TIME I'M IN THE CASTLE!

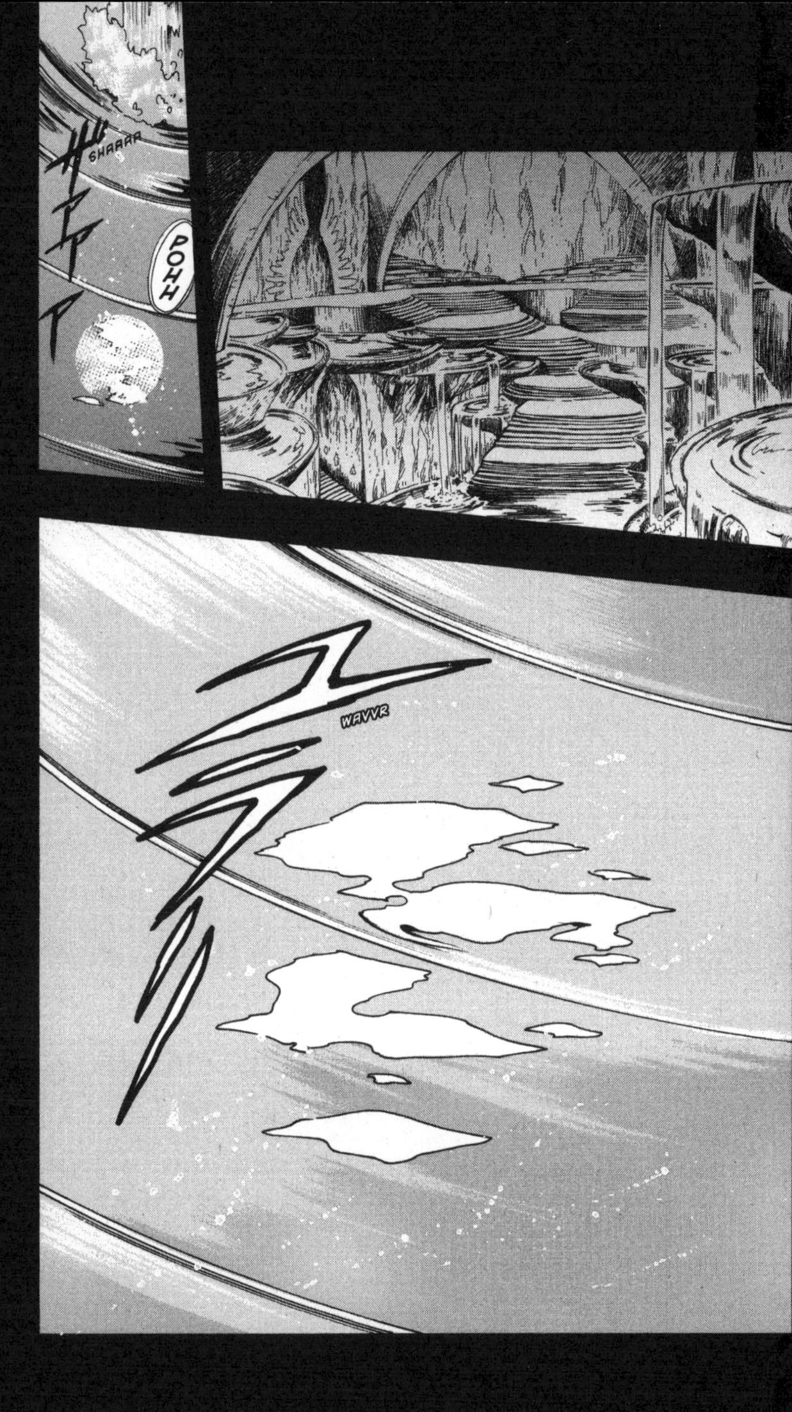
SHARRR
POHH
WAVVR

To Be Continued

About the Creators

CLAMP is a group of four women who have become the most popular manga artists in America—Nanase Ohkawa, Mokona, Satsuki Igarashi, and Tsubaki Nekoi. They started out as *doujinshi* (fan comics) creators, but their skill and craft brought them to the attention of publishers very quickly. Their first work from a major publisher was *RG Veda*, but their first mass success was with *Magic Knight Rayearth*. From there, they went on to write many series, including Cardcaptor Sakura and Chobits, two of the most popular manga in the United States. Like many Japanese manga artists, they prefer to avoid the spotlight, and little is known about them personally.

CLAMP is currently publishing three series in Japan: Tsubasa and xxxHOLiC with Kodansha and Gohou Drug with Kadokawa.

Translation Notes

Japanese is a tricky language for most Westerners, and translation is often more art than science. For your edification and reading pleasure, here are notes on some of the places where we could have gone in a different direction in our translation of the work, or where a Japanese cultural reference is used.

Par-yu, page 36

As has been mentioned in notes from previous volumes, when names or titles (or in this case, food names) come up spelled in *katakana* (the Japanese "alphabet" usually reserved for foreign words) with no Western spelling, the translator must choose a spelling that seems to fit the situation. In this case the word was *paayu*. The elongated "a" sound often indicates an "r" sound in the word. Quite a few other spellings are available, but this one (at least for me) seemed to fit the word best.

Purification, page 72

Although ritual purification rites in Japan are not full-body purifications in pools of water (as in Sakura's case), most large Japanese temples and shrines have places for ritual purification. The spots on the temple/shrine grounds are troughs, usually made of stone, of running water with wooden dippers placed in a row above the water. The rules of the custom vary from place to place, but in all cases, one dips the dipper into the water and pours it over one's hands. Other customs include drinking or quickly washing one's mouth with the water. Since these spots can be found in the majority of large temples and shrines in Japan, nearly everyone raised in Japan would be familiar with purification rites.

Mother-sama, Father-sama, Brother-sama, page 144

In fiction, the Imperial family and other rich or well-placed families tend to call one another by their family title followed by the -sama honorific. This is meant to be a show of respect, but it also gives off a nuance of people growing up in a privileged world apart from normal life.

Puria, Cocotto, page 158

In much the same way as explained in the note on par-yu, these are more food names spelled in *katakana* and left for the translator to find an appropriate spelling. I did my best based on the Japanese pronunciation. It is always possible that a different, official spelling for these dishes will be released by CLAMP after the publication of this book. If that happens, Del Rey will make every effort to correct this book's spelling in reprints.

Can I call you Syaoran?, page 161

To Western ears, this sounds like a strange question. In Western nations, if a person introduces himself by his first name only, it is implied that one has permission to use that name. But in Japan, one does not use honorifics when saying one's own name in a self-introduction, so when using the name, the other person adds an honorific to it. Sakura is actually asking if she can leave off the honorific when calling Syaoran by name—an intimacy reserved only for family and close friends. It means she wants to become close to Syaoran.

STORY BY KEN AKAMATSU
ART BY TAKUYA FUJIMA

BASED ON THE POPULAR ANIME!

Negi Springfield is only ten years old, but he's already a powerful wizard. After graduating from his magic school in England, the prodigy is given an unusual assignment: teach English at an all-girl school in Japan. Now Negi has to find a way to deal with his thirty-one totally gorgeous (and completely overaffectionate) students—without using magic! Based on the *Negima!* anime, this is a fresh take on the beloved *Negima!* story.

Available anywhere books or comics are sold!

VISIT WWW.DELREYMANGA.COM TO:

- Read sample pages
- View release date calendars for upcoming volumes
- Sign up for Del Rey's free manga e-newsletter
- Find out the latest about new Del Rey Manga series

DEL REY DEL REY MANGA

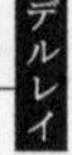

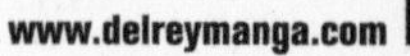

TOMARE!

[STOP!]

You're going the wrong way!

Manga is a completely different type of reading experience.

To start at the *beginning*, go to the *end*!

That's right! Authentic manga is read the traditional Japanese way—from right to left. Exactly the *opposite* of how American books are read. It's easy to follow: Just go to the other end of the book, and read each page—and each panel—from right side to left side, starting at the top right. Now you're experiencing manga as it was meant to be!